Imagination
WORKS!

101 Fun-Filled Reproducible Activities That Boost
Kids' Creative and Critical-Thinking Skills

by
Richard Porteus

SCHOLASTIC
PROFESSIONAL BOOKS

New York ◉ Toronto ◉ London ◉ Auckland ◉ Sydney

Mexico City ◉ New Delhi ◉ Hong Kong

To Carolyn, my wife,
whose support is endless.
—R.P.

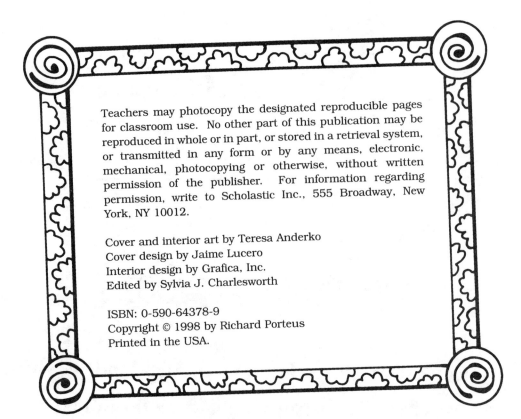

Cover and interior art by Teresa Anderko
Cover design by Jaime Lucero
Interior design by Grafica, Inc.
Edited by Sylvia J. Charlesworth

ISBN: 0-590-64378-9
Copyright © 1998 by Richard Porteus
Printed in the USA.

Table of Contents

Welcome to Imagination Works!

It's a dull, rainy Monday, and you wish you had a way to jump-start your class. You do! Hand out some of the forty reproducible pages in this book and your students will be off and running. Conversely, you've got some time before dismissal and the children are restive. What to do? Whip out *Imagination Works!*, and give them a chance to channel their energy creatively. Or, a few students have completed their assignments ahead of the class, and are looking around for something to do. *Imagination Works!* Perhaps you want to reward some students for a job well done. Reward them with a page (or pages) from *Imagination Works!*

But these are not the only ways you can use this book. Although most pages contain a number of ideas designed to free up thinking and encourage originality without a particular theme or absolute answers, there are some pages that can be used as a basis for a lesson. For example, one page has four activities related to food which could be used to start a discussion on healthful eating; another about school sports could lead to a lesson on good sportsmanship. Any one activity can be the foundation for any number of teaching topics—alliteration, poetry, vocabulary, math puzzles, and so on. There really are no limits for the uses of *Imagination Works!*

However, this book was designed mainly to stimulate students individually and to nurture their imaginations—using art, writing, math, music, and fantasy. There is even one activity relating to dance! As mentioned before, only a few projects require "correct" answers. You may choose to give everyone in the classroom the same sheet. Or all different ones. Then compare and discuss. Maybe you'd like to form groups to brainstorm together. Perhaps a student would like to do the same page more than once, or skip an activity or two. You're the teacher and can best decide what is right for your particular classroom. We're enthusiastic about this book and are sure you and your students will be, too. *Imagination Works!* will be an effective tool to help your whole class think and express itself in an atmosphere of fun and creativity. Enjoy!

Name _____

Imagination
WORKS!

Design a
pattern for this
tie.

List five new uses
for packing peanuts.

1. _____
2. _____
3. _____
4. _____
5. _____

If A=1, B=2, C=3 and so on,
can you name a day of the
week whose name adds up to
exactly 100? Write it on the
line.

_____

What's this zebra saying?
Fill her speech balloon.

Name _____

You have five toothpicks. Draw as many designs as you can using all five.

This is a cough.

Draw a hiccup.

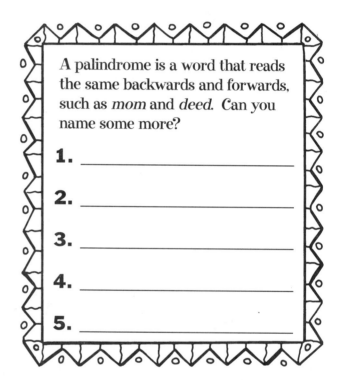

A palindrome is a word that reads the same backwards and forwards, such as *mom* and *deed*. Can you name some more?

1. _____

2. _____

3. _____

4. _____

5. _____

What did the dog say to make the doctor laugh?

Name ____________________

Make up a mini-story about haircuts.

Draw a butterfly using the initials of your name.

What do you think is behind this tree? Draw it peeking out.

What kind of dancing do you think these lines represent?

Name _____

Use these four words in any order in one sentence.

TIME   TELEPHONE   CAKE   LOCK

_____

_____

Decorate this bird.

You have hidden a treasure. Draw a map so your friend can find it.

Think up a new comic book character. Give it a name and describe it.

_____

CHARACTER NAME

_____

_____

_____

_____

_____

_____

_____

_____

_____

Name _____

Imagination WORKS!

Design a dwelling using these shapes as often as you want to.

Draw a face using the initials of your name.

Ebenezer Scrooge was very stingy. Can you name a person who is:

Courageous? _____

Athletic? _____

Beautiful? _____

Big? _____

Scary? _____

What is lonely cat singing about?

_____

_____

_____

_____

_____

_____

Name _____

Design a pendant for this necklace.

What is it? Write your answer on the lines.

_____

_____

_____

_____

You and your friends have a band. What is its name? What kind of music do you play?

_____

_____

_____

_____

MCM XVII LXXVI

In Roman numerals
II = 2
What is III? _____
C = 100
What is CC? _____
MM = 2,000
What is M? _____
X = 10
What is XXI? _____
Try to write your age in Roman numerals.

_____

DCCIV MV MMDC

Scholastic Professional Books

Imagination
WORKS!

Name: _____

The President of the United States is coming to your school for lunch. Decide what is on the menu, and write it below.

★ * * MENU * * ★

★ _____

★ _____

★ _____

★ _____

★ _____

★ _____

Fill in the balloons. What is he saying? What is she saying?

Ask someone for food to eat using picture symbols and letters, but no words.

Think up six new toppings for pizza. Draw one on each slice.

Imagination WORKS!

Name _____

Your computer needs a screen saver. Design it yourself.

What's for dinner? Draw your meal.

This frame needs a monster. Draw it.

Where is the bird taking him? Write your answer.

_____

_____

_____

_____

_____

_____

_____

Imagination WORKS!

Name _____

Design a stamp celebrating your hero.

U.S.A.

_____ ¢

"W" is sometimes called double "U." Give these letters nicknames!

B _____

H _____

Q _____

X _____

Continue the patterns.

AB, BCC, CD, _____
_____

10, 1; 9, 2; 8, _____
_____

a, be, cup, _____
_____

mouse, cat, cat, dog, dog, dog, _____
_____

bad, good; up, down; _____
_____

What is the poodle saying to the artist?

Imagination
WORKS!

Name _____

Decorate this butterfly!

I'd like to be a(n)

_____

(name of animal)

because...

_____

_____

_____

Make faces on these balloons.

Create an animal by coloring any
number of shapes.

Imagination WORKS!

Name: _____

There is a knock on your door. You open it. A visitor from outer space stands there. Draw it and fill in the speech balloon.

Which do you think takes up more space in your body, a tickle or a pain? Why?

_____
_____
_____
_____
_____
_____

Decorate me.

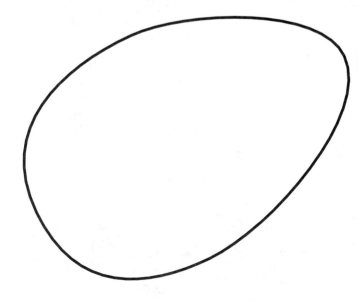

Fill in the blanks.

Seed is to plant,

as _____ is to chicken,

as nut is to _____,

as _____ is to sea,

as note is to _____,

as _____ is to sentence.

Imagination
WORKS!

Name _____

Fill in the speech balloon.

Put adjectives before these nouns.
We did the first one for you!

troubling _____ **tarantula**

_____ **piranha**

_____ **koala**

_____ **penguin**

_____ **giraffe**

_____ **toad**

Draw an animal that has stripes and spots, rounded ears, a bent tail, BIG eyes, and funny looking legs. Name it!

Name: _____

Create an advertising jingle for your favorite zoo.

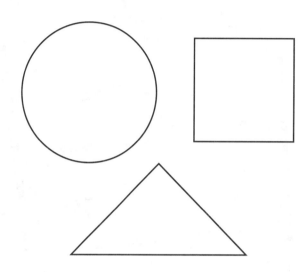

Imagination WORKS!

Name _____

Draw these words to look like what they mean.

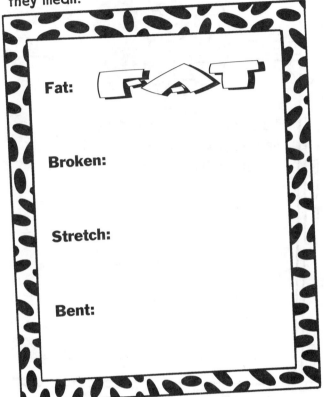

Fat: **FAT**

Broken:

Stretch:

Bent:

Fit your three initials inside these shapes.

Make up a silly rhyme:

Said the dentist while drilling...

_____

_____

_____

_____

_____

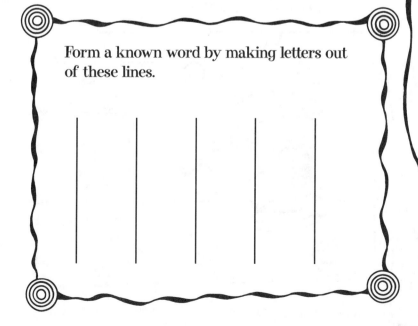

Form a known word by making letters out of these lines.

Imagination WORKS!

Name _____

Make up five wacky names for bubble gum flavors.

1. _____
2. _____
3. _____
4. _____
5. _____

Your country is sending you on a secret mission. In a few lines describe it.

_____
_____
_____
_____
_____
_____

Design a mini web site for your school.

"GeEble Pople doOp gRunch aZeby"

Respond to the alien in his language.

Imagination
WORKS!

Name _____

You have your own personal robot. Draw it, name it, and tell what it does for you.

NAME

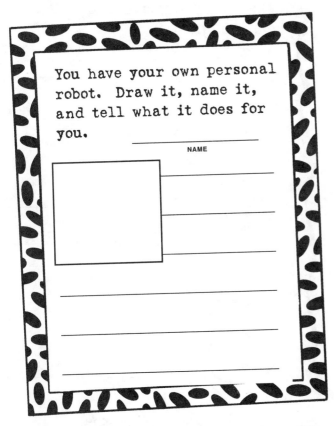

Fill in these speech balloons:

Why does she smile? Why does she frown? Draw your answer.

Design a number to go between 5 and 6.

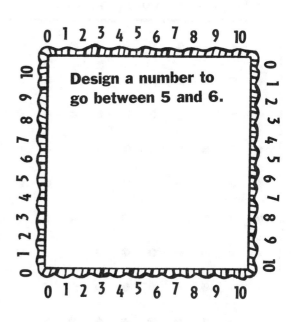

Scholastic Professional Books

Imagination
WORKS!

Name _____

Make up a game to be played with a pinecone and chopsticks. The object of the game is:

_____
_____
_____
_____
_____

What do these signs mean. Use your imagination.

_____
_____

_____
_____

_____
_____

Make a design on this geo-board.

Lion is to pride; as elephant is

to _____; as goose is to

_____; as _____ is to

school; as ant is to _____;

as _____ is to hive.

20

Imagination
WORKS!

Name _____

What is behind this sign?
Draw it.

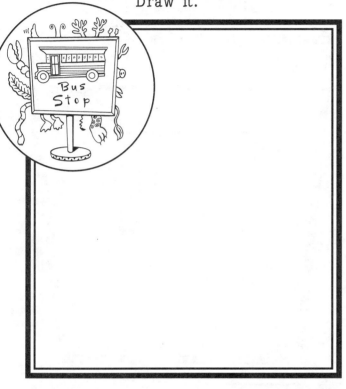

Which do you think would weigh
more. Why?

A or 1

_____

_____

_____

_____

_____

_____

Play match-up! We did the first
one for you.

Soccer	**Football**
Bulls-eye	**Basketball**
Baseball	**Tennis**
Quarter-back	**Goalie**
Slam-dunk	**Diamond**
Love	**Archery**

What is he
saying?

Imagination **WORKS!**

Name _____

What helpful hint is she giving him?

Create an e-mail to send to a pen pal on Mars.

List five problems in your community that need working on.

_____

_____

_____

_____

_____

You have been asked to come up with a nickname, flower, bird, and motto for your town or city.

nickname _____

flower _____

bird _____

motto _____

_____

_____

22

Imagination
WORKS!

Name _____

Connect enough dots
to make a face.

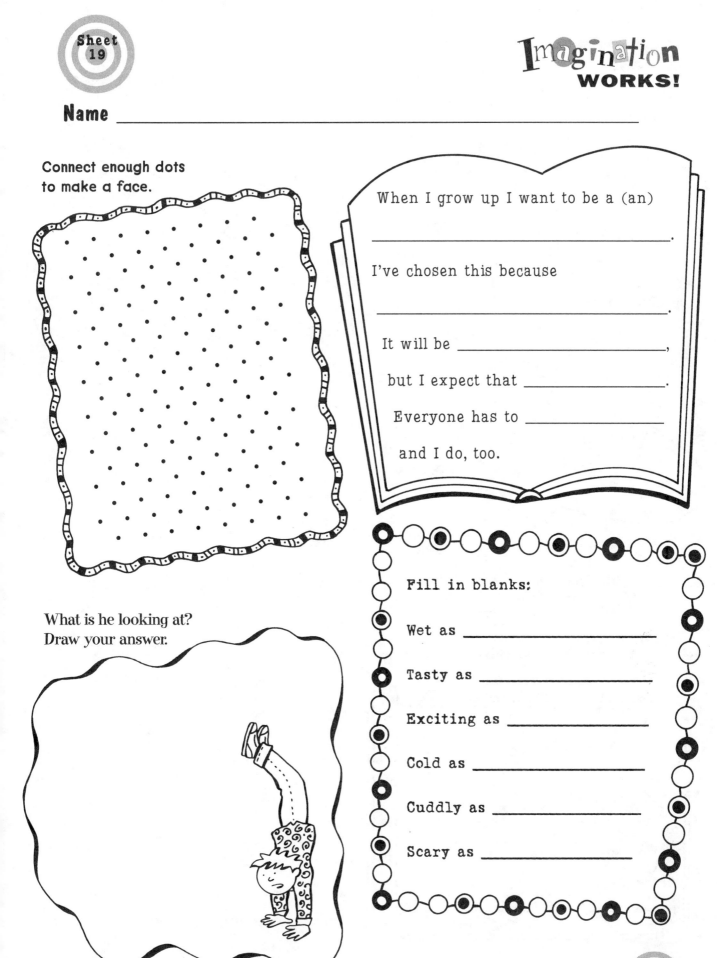

When I grow up I want to be a (an)

_____.

I've chosen this because

_____.

It will be _____,

but I expect that _____.

Everyone has to _____

and I do, too.

What is he looking at?
Draw your answer.

Fill in blanks:

Wet as _____

Tasty as _____

Exciting as _____

Cold as _____

Cuddly as _____

Scary as _____

Imagination
WORKS!

Name _____

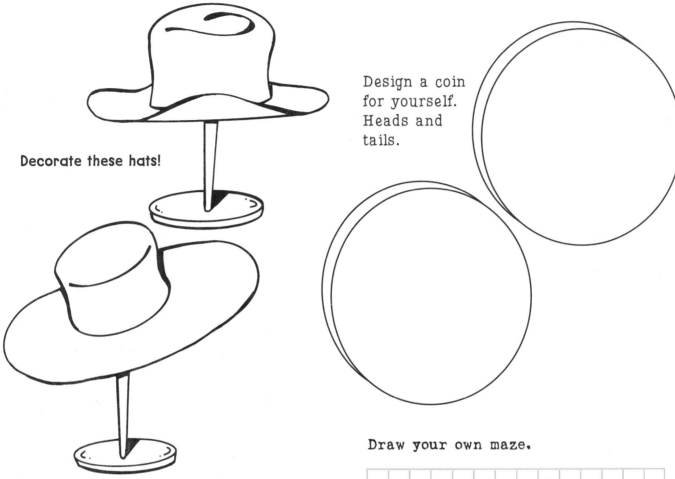

Decorate these hats!

Design a coin
for yourself.
Heads and
tails.

Draw your own maze.

Tell some things you can do with ice cream sticks.

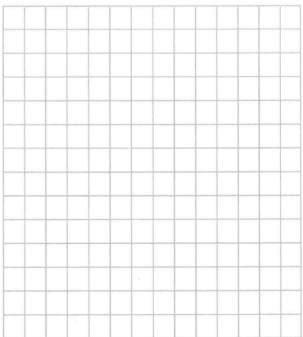

24

Imagination WORKS!

Name _____

Make this egg into a clown face.

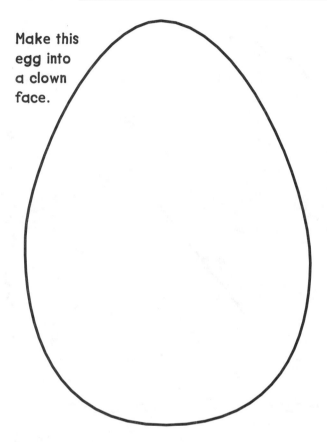

I would like to be the letter

_____ because...

_____
_____
_____
_____
_____

How many words can you make if you scramble the letters of your last name?

Name: _____
_____
_____
_____
_____
_____
_____

Connect the outer two numbers and put the sum in middle; now do the next two numbers, and so on.... What is the lucky number?

1 2 3 4 5 6 7

Imagination
WORKS!

Name _____

Fill in the blank squares with a missing number from 1-9 (used only once) so each set of three (up and down) adds up to 15.

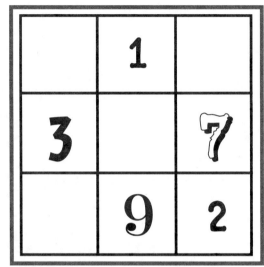

Use this line to draw a picture.

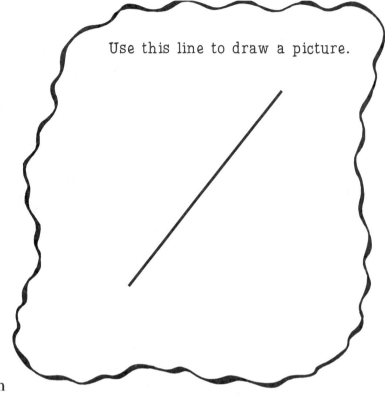

Write a four line poem with lines ending in fake, make, shake, and cake in any order.

_____ .

_____

_____

_____

Create weather icons for the following situations:

A sunny day.

Day with thunderstorm.

A snowy day.

Very windy day.

Imagination WORKS!

Name _____

Fill in the missing letters in matching script.

a b c _ e f g _
h i J k l _ n
o _ q r s t u
r w _ y z a b
C D E _ G H I
J K L _ N O P Q
r s t u v w _ Y S

Draw a stop sign without using the word "stop."

Draw a lazy line meeting a nervous line.

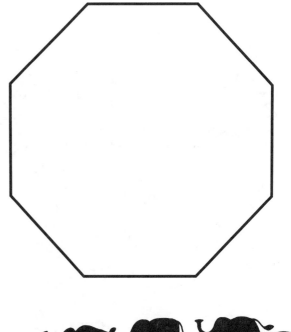

Draw a line between the words that are related.

arachnid   **snake**

venom   **tentacles**

octopus   **reptile**

marsupial   **spider**

dinosaur   **kangaroo**

Imagination WORKS!

Name _____

What are they saying?
Fill in the speech balloons.

Draw and name your own vehicle for inter-planetary travel.

Give this dog a name.
Write it on his tag.

Write in a few sentences about a time "you saved the day."

_____
_____
_____
_____
_____

28

Sheet
25

Imagination
WORKS!

Name _____

Draw hair on these heads.

Make a silly rhyme.
Said the sailor to the whale...

_____

_____

_____

_____

Name five (or more) musical instruments
you can make from items in your kitchen.

_____
_____
_____
_____
_____

Write a mini story
about this line.

_____
_____
_____
_____
_____
_____

Imagination
WORKS!

Name _____

Design your own family flag.

What color are you?
_____

What season?
_____

What geographical feature?
_____

What song?
_____

What plant?
_____

What animal?
_____

What vehicle?
_____

Use your first name to write
an acrostic poem.

It's your birthday.
You can go anywhere you want.
Where are you going and why?

_____

_____

_____

_____

30

WORKS!

Name _____

Design a team shirt for **your** school.

Make up a school cheer.

_____

_____

_____

_____

_____

_____

Here is my recipe for a champion.

_____

_____

_____

_____

_____

_____

Put these words in the right category below: Touch-down, 3-pointer, goal, homer, hole-in-one.

Golf _____

Hockey _____

Baseball _____

Basketball _____

Football _____

Imagination WORKS!

Name _____

Design a wonderfully wacky birdhouse.

What are they saying?
Fill in the speech balloons.

Finish drawing these birds and name them!

Make up 5 song titles with animal names in them. We did the first one for you.

The Big, Bad, Oh-So-Blue Bull Frog

_____

_____

_____

_____

_____

Name _____

Design a new
candy bar
wrapper.

Ingredients:

Jlluminate your first name. (This means making the first letter very large and
very fancy like the I in *Illuminate*.)

Write the numbers 1 through 9 across
the page. On the second line reverse
the numbers. Repeat first two lines.
Now add a 2 on the far right as the
fifth line. Add all five lines. What do
you get? Does it work for "3"? "1"?

_____
_____
_____
_____
_____

Complete this message...

"Get well quick, I..."

_____
_____
_____
_____
_____

Imagination WORKS!

Name _____

Draw something in or on each hand.

Make up two bumper stickers promoting two things you believe in.

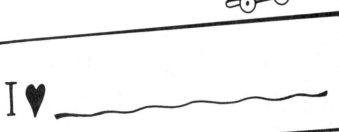

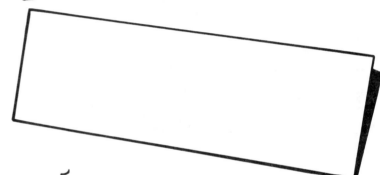

I ♥ _____

What is she saying?

I would like to be the number ____ because . . .

34

Scholastic Professional Books

Name _____

Can you recognize these words without their "eyes"? See if you can write them correctly.

nnng _____

Msssspp _____

ce _____

sp _____

cmg _____

ble _____

rresstble _____

Draw a bouquet for this vase.

My favorite flower is a

_____

because . . .

_____

_____

_____

_____

The weather service names hurricanes. Agnes was a very severe hurricane. Now you name a tornado, an ice storm, a sand storm, an earthquake, a flood, and a blizzard.

tornado _____

ice storm _____

sand storm _____

earthquake _____

flood _____

blizzard _____

Imagination WORKS!

Name _____

Use these familiar marks any way you want and as many times as you want to fill in the faces below.

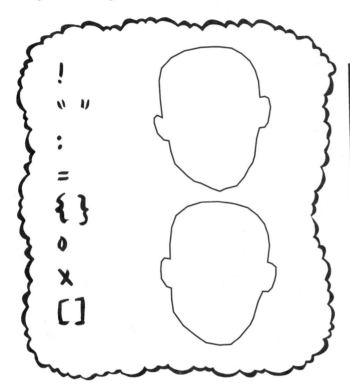

Fill in with an animal.

Quiet as a _____

Sly as a _____

Wise as a(n) _____

Busy as a _____

Stubborn as a _____

Draw what you see through this window.

Draw a delicious dessert here and then give it a name!

_____

_____

Name

Imagination WORKS!

Name _____

You want to say something original on your answering machine message. What's it going to be?

Does yellow make you happy? Draw a rainbow and next to each color tell how that color makes you feel.

Can you name five songs that mention colors?

1. _____

2. _____

3. _____

4. _____

5. _____

My favorite color is

_____

because . . .

Imagination
WORKS!

Name _____

Cross out what doesn't belong on each line.

1. Help, 911, SOS, ambulance

2. Carrots, peaches, corn, asparagus

3. Monkey, wolf, whale, giraffe

4. Sing, dance, run, jump

5. Bacon, beef, broccoli, cheese

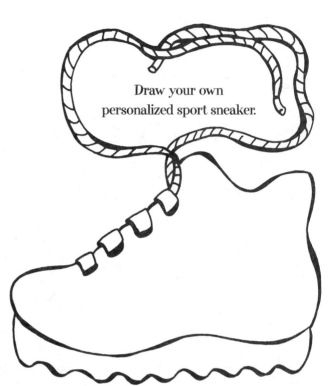

Draw your own personalized sport sneaker.

Make word clues for this crossword puzzle.

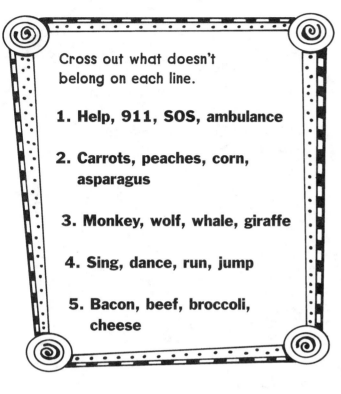

Across

1. _____

2. _____

Down

1. _____

2. _____

3. _____

Draw yourself enjoying your favorite season.

Name _____

Show this tree in all four seasons.

Here are two houses. You are the architect. Make each one attractive and different.

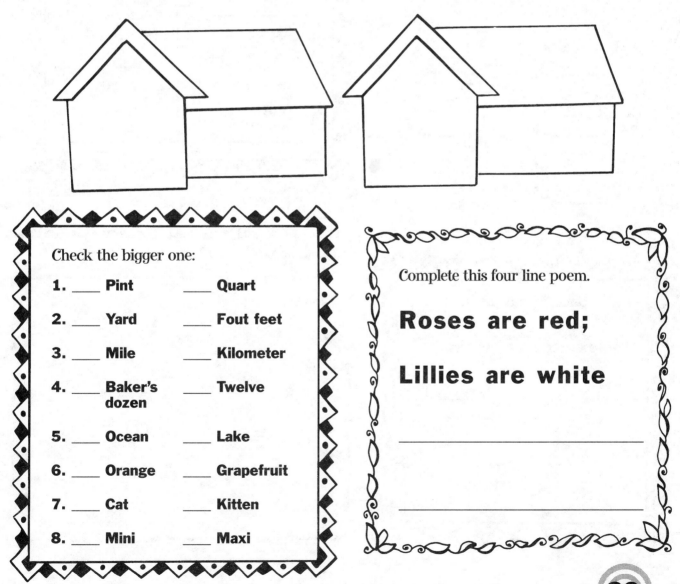

Check the bigger one:

1. ___ Pint   ___ Quart

2. ___ Yard   ___ Fout feet

3. ___ Mile   ___ Kilometer

4. ___ Baker's   ___ Twelve
       dozen

5. ___ Ocean   ___ Lake

6. ___ Orange   ___ Grapefruit

7. ___ Cat   ___ Kitten

8. ___ Mini   ___ Maxi

Complete this four line poem.

Roses are red;

Lillies are white

_____

_____

39

Imagination **WORKS!**

Name _____

A shy potted plant has met a confident potted plant. Draw them talking to each other (use speech balloons).

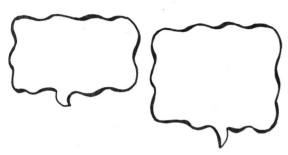

Cross out the one that is not correct:

1/2	16 oz.
50 cents	2 cups
4/8	18
75%	8+8

10 cents	one third
$1.00	$\frac{4}{12}$
one hundred	5:10
C (Roman numeral)	3 out of 9

Write in the two missing lines.

There once was a teacher,

Whose outstanding feature,

_____

_____

Like no other creature.

This is a welcome mat for your school. What does it say?

Imagination WORKS!

Name _____

You are around the campfire with your friends. It is your turn to start a scary story. Write your first three sentences.

Safety first! Draw a line between the matches.

Bicycle	**Fire drill**
Life jacket	**Beach**
Sun screen	**Seat belt**
School	**Boat**
Automobile	**Helmet**
Runner	**Flourescent patches**

Your job is to create a monster for the scariest movie ever. Draw it and name it.

My favorite holiday is

_____.

I celebrate by _____

_____

_____

_____

_____.

Imagination
WORKS!

Name _____

Draw the front of the postcard you are
sending your best friend. Now do the
message part.

_____
_____
_____   TO:
_____
_____

Try to draw an outline
map of your state from
memory. Show the
capital, where you live,
and anything else you
want to.

Fill in the blanks:

I live in the state of

_____.

The biggest city near me is

_____.

The thing I like best about where I live is

_____.

My state is famous for

_____.

Something historical about my area is

_____.

If I move, I want to go to

_____.

42

Imagination WORKS!

Name _____

You are writing a book with two animal characters. Name them and describe them.

Name _____   **Name** _____

_____   _____
_____   _____
_____   _____
_____   _____
_____   _____
_____   _____

Design the front and back of a new dollar bill.

Weeping willow and toothless Tom are alliterations. Can you think up four more?

1. _____
_____

2. _____
_____

3. _____
_____

4. _____
_____

_____
_____
_____

Igpay atinlay is pig Latin for "pig Latin." Try to write a simple sentence in pig Latin.

Imagination WORKS!

Name _____

Make people out of these letters.

A O P

D T X

Finish each sentence.

A hug is like a _____.

A laugh is like a _____.

A tear is like a _____.

Clouds are like _____.

Trees are like _____.

See if you can unscramble these words to make vegetables:

Artcor _____

Crobcoil _____

mattoo _____

tebe _____

eap _____

Think up five ingredients for a witch's brew.

_____

_____

_____

_____

Scholastic Professional Books

Name _____

Design your own *Imagination Works!* sheet for a friend.

Name _____

Design your own *Imagination Works!* sheet for a friend.

Name _____

Design your own *Imagination Works!* sheet for a friend.

ABOUT THE AUTHOR

Richard Porteus is now retired, but was a public school teacher for nearly forty years. In addition to such a full career in the classroom, he has designed jewelry, painted murals, and he does graphic design and cartooning. He is a published author with texts covering subjects from math to cats. Busier than ever creating arts and crafts with his grandchildren and others, he is someone who knows how to think creatively. Better yet, he knows how to encourage others to make their imaginations work!